ANCIENT TRADITIONS, MODERN MINDS

THE EVOLUTION OF INDIAN SPIRITUALITY IN THE 21ST CENTURY

DR. JAGADEESH PILLAI

Made with ♥ on the Notion Press Platform
www.notionpress.com

|| "Dedicated to all who seek to understand and
appreciate Indian culture and tradition." ||

Contents

Contents

Prayer

"Om Sahanaa Vavatu Sahanau BhunaktuSaha Veeryam KaravaavahaiTejasvi Naavadheetamastu Maa VidvishaavahaiOm Shantih Shantih Shantih"

The literal interpretation of this mantra is: OM. Let us all protect one another, let us all share in joy, let us all work together and let our learning be illuminated. Let us be united in peace,
OM Peace, Peace, Peace

ᎮᎮᎮ

About The Author

Dr. Jagadeesh Pillai is a renowned Guinness World Record holder, writer, and researcher hailing from Varanasi, also known as the abode of Lord Shiva. With a Ph.D. in Vedic Science and a range of creative ideas and achievements, he is a true polymath. He is the author of more than 100 books including Research Publications. Although his roots can be traced back to Kerala, the people of Varanasi hold him in high regard and affectionately consider him one of their own.

Dr. Pillai has achieved four Guinness World Records in the following subjects:

"Script to Screen" - In this record, Dr. Pillai produced and directed an animation film within the shortest time possible, breaking the previous record set by Canadians. He has also received numerous national and international awards and recognitions for this achievement.

Longest Line of Postcards - For this record, Dr. Pillai created a line of 16,300 postcards on the occasion of the 163rd anniversary of Indian Postal Day. The event also included a questionnaire about the Indian flag.

Largest Poster Awareness Campaign - Dr. Pillai designed an awareness campaign on the subject of "Beti Bachao - Beti Padhao" (Save the Girl Child - Educate the Girl Child) to achieve this record.

Largest Envelope - In tribute to the Indian Prime Minister's

"Make in India" initiative, Dr. Pillai created a 4000 square meter envelope using waste paper to achieve this record.

Attempted - **70000 Candles on a 210 kg Cake** - To celebrate the 70th Indian Independence Day, Dr. Pillai attempted to light 70,000 candles on a 210 kg cake, which was recorded in World Records India.

Attempted - **Documentary on Dhamek Stupa of Sarnath in 17 Languages** - Dr. Pillai attempted to create a documentary on the Dhamek Stupa of Sarnath, dubbing it in 17 different languages. The result of this attempt is currently awaiting confirmation from the Guinness World Records.

Dr. Pillai is skilled in teaching the Bhagavad Gita, a Hindu scripture, and is popular among young people. He has helped many young people improve their lives through his motivational teachings.

In addition to teaching, he has composed and sung numerous Sanskrit Bhajans and patriotic songs.

He has also written and directed several short films and documentaries for awareness campaigns, and has volunteered with the police in both UP and Kerala to spread awareness about various issues through videos and photography.

Incredibly, he has produced and directed over 100 documentaries about the city of Varanasi, all on his own.

He has also helped and guided more than 25 boys and girls to achieve world records through creative and innovative methods. He is a multifaceted person who uses his intellect and the blessings given to him by God to excel in various areas. He is both a teacher and a student, always learning and teaching, and is able to master any subject he comes across.

He is a selfless social activist and motivational speaker who has overcome struggles and failures to become a successful and enthusiastic individual with a rich life experience.

In addition to his work with the Bhagavad Gita, he is also an efficient Tarot card reader, Astro-Vastu consultant, and a talented singer and composer. He has sung the entire Ram Charita Manas and Bhagavad Gita in his own compositions, and has sung the phrase "Lokah Samastha Sukhino Bhavantu" in 50 different languages. He is currently working on a detailed and scientific study of Vedas, Upanishads, Puranas, and the Bhagavad Gita. He has also composed and sung the Hanuman Chalisa and Gayatri Mantra in 108 and 1008 different compositions, respectively.

Awards - Four Times Guinness World Records, Winner of Mahatma Gandhi Vishwa Shanti Puraskar, Mahatma Gandhi Global Peace Ambassador, Kashi Ratna Award, Dr. APJ Abdul Kalam Motivational Person of the Year 2017, Mother Teresa Award, Indira Gandhi Priyadarshini Award, Bharat Vikas Ratna Award, Udyog Ratna Award, Vigyan Prasar Award, Poorvanchal Ratn Samman.

ॐॐॐ

Preface

In "Ancient Traditions, Modern Minds: The Evolution of Indian Spirituality in the 21st Century," we explore the dynamic evolution of Indian spirituality in the context of a rapidly changing world. From ancient spiritual practices to modern interpretations and adaptations, this book delves into the ways in which Indian spirituality has evolved to meet the needs of a new generation.

India has a rich spiritual heritage that spans thousands of years. From the Vedic period to the Bhakti movement and beyond, Indian spirituality has played a central role in shaping the culture and way of life of the people of India. However, with the advent of the 21st century, we are witnessing a profound shift in the way that Indian spirituality is understood and practiced.

The 21st century has brought with it a host of new challenges, from rapid urbanization and globalization to the explosion of new technologies and the rise of social media. As a result, traditional spiritual practices and beliefs are being called into question as people search for new ways to connect with the divine and find meaning in their lives.

At the same time, we are also seeing a renewed interest in Indian spirituality among people from all walks of life. From Westerners seeking to deepen their understanding of Eastern philosophy to Indians looking to reconnect with their cultural heritage, there is a growing curiosity about the wisdom and practices of the past.

"Ancient Traditions, Modern Minds" explores these trends and more, examining the ways in which Indian spirituality is being adapted and reimagined in the 21st century. Through in-depth interviews with spiritual leaders and practitioners, as well as a close examination of contemporary spiritual movements and practices, this book offers a unique and thought-provoking look at the evolution of Indian spirituality in the 21st century.

This book is a must-read for anyone interested in understanding the spiritual landscape of India today and the ways in which ancient traditions are being adapted to meet the needs of modern minds. It is a journey of discovery for readers of all backgrounds, as it delves into the diverse spiritual practices and beliefs that have shaped the Indian culture.

In short, "Ancient Traditions, Modern Minds" is a fascinating exploration of how Indian spirituality is evolving to meet the needs of the 21st century, and how it continues to shape the culture and way of life of the people of India.

$$\rhd\rhd\rhd$$

ONE

THE GLOBALIZATION OF YOGA: THE EVOLUTION OF AN ANCIENT PRACTICE

India, the land of spiritualism and ancient traditions, has been a hotbed for spiritual practices for centuries. Yoga, one of the most ancient practices, has been an integral part of Indian culture for thousands of years. However, in recent times, with the rise of globalization and the growing interest in Eastern spiritual practices, yoga has become a global phenomenon. In this chapter, we will explore the evolution of Indian spirituality in the 21st century and how the globalization of yoga has played a significant role in it.

The 21st century has seen a significant increase in the popularity of yoga and other spiritual practices in India and around the world. Yoga, which originated in India, has become one of the most popular forms of exercise and spiritual practice in the world. The growing interest in yoga has led to a significant increase in the number of yoga practitioners, teachers, and studios worldwide.

The globalization of yoga has had a profound impact on Indian spirituality. The spread of yoga has led to an increased interest in Indian spiritual practices and culture, and many people from around the world are now seeking to learn about Indian spirituality. This has led to an increased demand for authentic Indian spiritual experiences and teachings. As a result, many spiritual leaders and teachers in India have started to offer spiritual retreats, workshops, and other programs to cater to the growing demand from foreign tourists and spiritual seekers.

The globalization of yoga has also led to the emergence of new forms of yoga that are more accessible to Westerners. Many yoga teachers and studios have started to offer more modern and Westernized forms of yoga, such as power yoga, hot yoga, and yoga for weight loss. These forms of yoga are designed to appeal to Westerners and are more focused on physical fitness and wellness rather than spiritual development.

In addition to the growth of new forms of yoga, the globalization of yoga has also led to an increased interest in other Indian spiritual practices such as meditation, Ayurveda, and Vedic astrology. Many people from around the world are now seeking to learn about these practices and integrate them into their daily lives. This has led to an increased demand for authentic Indian spiritual experiences and teachings in these areas as well.

However, the globalization of yoga has also led to some challenges for Indian spirituality. One of the main challenges has been the commercialization of yoga and other spiritual practices. Many yoga teachers and studios have started to focus on making money rather than providing authentic spiritual experiences. This has led to a proliferation of unqualified teachers and fake spiritual gurus who are more interested in making money than helping people to develop spiritually.

Another challenge has been the loss of cultural context in the globalization of yoga. Many Westerners have started to practice yoga without understanding its cultural and spiritual roots. This has led to a lack of understanding and appreciation for the deeper spiritual aspects of yoga.

Despite these challenges, the globalization of yoga has had a positive impact on Indian spirituality overall. The increased interest in yoga and other spiritual practices has led to a renewed appreciation for Indian spirituality and culture, and has helped to preserve and promote ancient spiritual practices in the modern world. Many spiritual leaders and teachers in India have also started to adapt their teachings and practices to better serve the growing demand from foreign tourists and spiritual seekers.

The globalization of yoga has played a significant role in the evolution of Indian spirituality in the 21st century. The spread of yoga has led to an increased interest in Indian spiritual practices and culture, and has helped to preserve and promote ancient spiritual practices in the modern world. However, the commercialization of yoga and the loss of cultural context have also presented challenges for Indian spirituality.

༄༄༄

"India is a land of contrasts, where the old and the new coexist in perfect harmony. This is a country where the past and the present coexist in perfect harmony." - Paul Theroux

TWO

THE RELEVANCE OF INDIAN SPIRITUALITY IN THE MODERN WORLD

India is a land of spirituality, its deep-rooted religious and philosophical traditions dating back thousands of years. Despite the erosion of its religious traditions following colonization, a resurgence of Indian spirituality has emerged in recent years, prompting many to recognize its relevance in today's modern world. Indian spirituality boasts a wide variety of methods and practices that seek to cultivate self-reflection, mindfulness and inner peace.

At the heart of Indian spirituality lies multiple religious traditions, most notably Hinduism and Buddhism. These systems of thought uphold the core tenet of understanding the Inner Self and its relationship to the physical world. Ideas such as karma and ahimsa are emphasized in both religions, placing a focus on finding balance between one's individual desires and the greater good of humanity. For instance, the doctrine of ahimsa promotes the practice of nonviolence in thought, speech, and action. When embraced, this facet of Indian spirituality can lead individuals to transcend our egocentric orientation and more fully understand the interconnectedness of life.

Further, the philosophy of advaita, which promotes the notion of nondualism, is integral to Indian spirituality. This practice is focused on the acknowledgement of the oneness of all living things and the ultimate divine reality that lies beyond our physical realm. This concept pushes us to move beyond the illusion of separateness and realize the inseparable unity of the universe. Such a belief inspires contemplation on our interconnectedness and leads us to behave towards others with humility and respect.

Additionally, certain meditational practices in Indian spirituality focus on cultivating the capacity of our minds. By developing the ability to observe thoughts without judgment or attachment, we can begin to distinguish between what is real and what is imagined. Through an attentive and reflective approach to our inner workings, we can more readily access our intuition and gain a greater understanding of the greater world around us.

Finally, Indian spirituality often comes with a commitment to self-care and active compassion. Common practices such as yoga, pranayama, and aromatherapy can be used to balance mind, body, and soul, creating physical and spiritual well-being. With an emphasis on self-love and respect for life, these practices nurture our capacity for compassion and build bridges between ourselves and the universe.

Indian spirituality provides us with a wide range of practices and principles that can bolster our connection to the world. By embracing its teachings, we can access a deeper understanding of who we are and how we can be valuable and responsible contributors to the lives of others.

ꗞꗞꗞ

"India is a land of ancient wisdom, where tradition and modernity coexist in perfect harmony." - J.K. Rowling

THREE

THE NEW AGE MOVEMENT AND INDIAN SPIRITUALITY: A SYNTHESIS OR AN APPROPRIATION

The New Age movement has been on the rise since the 1950s and has become a household term of sorts over the past several decades. It has been described as a spiritual movement and cultural shift occurring throughout the world and has been known to encompass some of the more fringe aspects of human spirituality. Indian Spirituality, on the other hand, has always been a cornerstone of Indian culture and has been practiced for centuries by Hindus, Sikhs, Buddhists and many more seekers of inner peace and fulfillment. There has been much debate over the years as to whether or not the two can be synthesized, with both sides having their own unique views.

The idea of synthesizing aspects of the New Age movement with Indian Spirituality has its supporters and detractors. Proponents of this idea argue that combining Western ideals with traditional Eastern practices can create a holistic form of spirituality that is deeply contextual, yet also relevant to modern-day life. For example, the use of yoga and meditation, which are practices common to Indian Spirituality, could be combined with creative visualizations and affirmations drawn from the New Age movement. This could provide an effective tool for aiding people in achieving life-changing spiritual transformation.

Conversely, those who are against this type of synthesis criticise the lack of understanding and appreciation for Indian Spirituality in the New Age movement. According to these critics, the New Age movement has diluted and adopted many of the spiritual practices of India without acknowledging the original source. This could lead to spiritual misrepresentation, misunderstanding, and a lack of respect for the centuries' old practices. In addition, critics of this synthesis argue that traditional Indian Spirituality and culture may be in danger of being hijacked by Western ideals, and are wary of the possibility of losing its true essence.

Ultimately, Indian Spirituality and the New Age movement can be synthesized depending on the individual and the context. When done through respectful dialogue, collaboration, and education, it can produce a unique blend of spiritual exploration and discovery. When done out of respect and appreciation for both cultures, and an understanding of the nuances of each practice, it can provide a truly enlightening experience for those seeking fulfilment and inner peace. Thus, the synthesis of New Age and Indian Spirituality can be seen as an opportunity for individuals to broaden and explore their spiritual horizons.

ᗡᗡᗡ

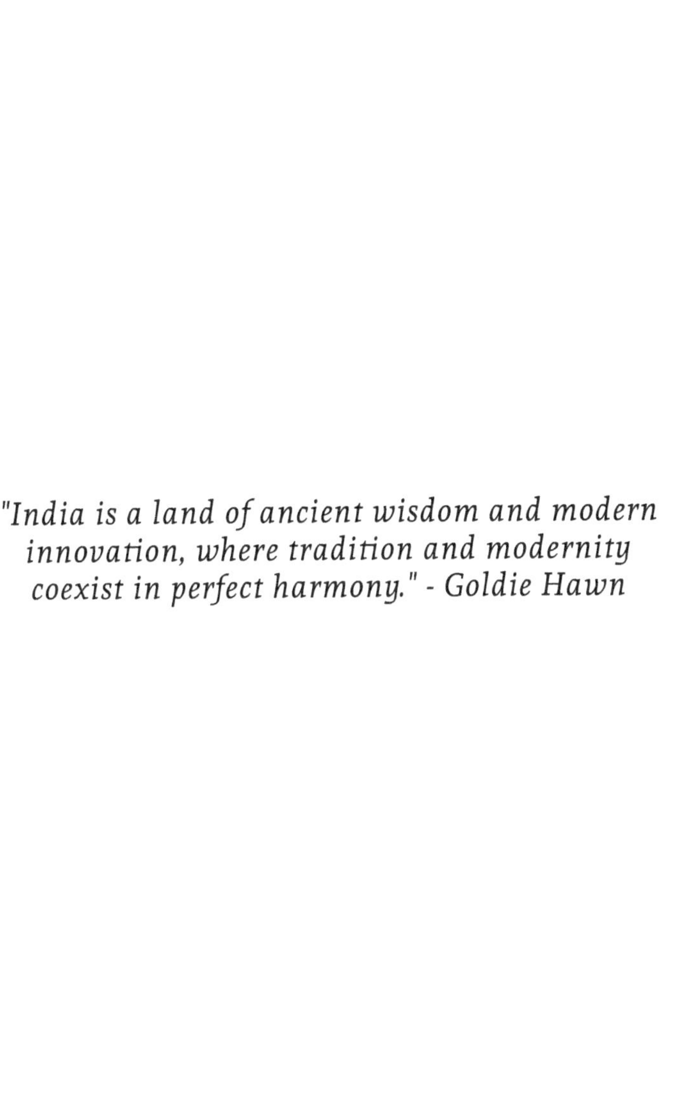

"India is a land of ancient wisdom and modern innovation, where tradition and modernity coexist in perfect harmony." - Goldie Hawn

FOUR

THE RISE OF MINDFULNESS: HOW EASTERN MEDITATION TECHNIQUES ARE CHANGING THE WEST

Since the dawn of civilization, Eastern meditation techniques have been used for physical, spiritual and mental transformation. Today, these techniques have crossed over into the West, radically changing the way we approach wellbeing. The global pandemic has heightened our need for stress relief, making Eastern meditation techniques more popular than ever.

The global wellness industry is a trillion-dollar sector that has been greatly impacted by Eastern meditation practices. Since the early 2000s, Westerners have been gravitating toward mindfulness, the practice of being present and aware of the moment. Mindfulness teachers in the West have been influenced by Eastern teachings such as Vipassana, which originated in ancient India. The West has also embraced yoga, an ancient practice originating in India that combines physical postures, breathing exercises and meditation.

The influence of Eastern meditation techniques is also being felt in the corporate world. Many companies are now offering mindfulness and meditation classes as part of their employee wellness programs. The purpose is to reduce stress, improve creativity and boost productivity. At the same time, Eastern techniques such as yoga and Tai Chi are being used to increase physical activity and strengthen team dynamics in the workplace.

Eastern meditation techniques are also being used to help people recover from trauma. Practices such as Somatic Experiencing and Eye Movement Desensitization & Reprocessing (EMDR) are rooted in Eastern approaches to mental and physical health. These techniques can be used to reduce symptoms of post-traumatic stress disorder, anxiety and depression.

Finally, Eastern mediation techniques are being used to support holistic healing in personal and professional settings. Practices such as yoga and meditation, which were once viewed as fringe, are now being embraced by the mainstream, thanks to their many proven health benefits. They are helping people to better handle stress, increase self-awareness and develop a more positive attitude towards life.

Eastern meditation techniques are changing the West in multiple ways. They have become integral to the global wellness industry, are being embraced by the corporate world, and are providing individuals with powerful tools for personal and professional transformation. Thanks to the growing popularity of these ancient, Eastern practices, the West is experiencing a much-needed revolution in the way it approaches wellbeing.

"India is a country of many languages and many religions, but it is also a country of many beautiful landscapes and many beautiful buildings." - Gustave Flaubert

FIVE

The Role of Technology in the Evolution of Indian Spirituality

Technology often gets a bad rap today, but in a society known for its spirituality, technology is playing an increasingly important role in the advancement of Indian spiritual life. It has become an integral part of the culture, offering many spiritual benefits that would make it difficult to truly engage in contemporary Indian spirituality without the help of technology.

The most pronounced example of this phenomenon is the ubiquity of video streaming and recorded religious ceremonies. For example, it has become commonplace to access video streams of religious ceremonies live or download them for future viewing. This makes it possible to watch sacred rituals from the comfort of one's own home - or from any other location. This means that those who cannot physically attend ceremonies can still gain spiritual insight, participating in initiations, hearing lectures, and being part of the ceremony without having to travel.

Technology has also greatly increased access to spiritual teachings, both modern and ancient. Many websites offer tutorials on topics ranging from meditation to yoga to Hindu scripture. There are also applications for smartphones and tablets providing users with daily reminders to meditate or practice yoga. In addition, users of these applications can easily access recorded lectures, either from teachers within their community or from other places around the world.

Technology has also made it possible to connect with mentors and spiritual teachers more easily. Sites like Skype and FaceTime make it possible to interact with religious leaders, ask questions, and gain insight into the wide range of spiritual practices and beliefs in India. This is especially important for those living far away from their teacher, as it helps close the geographical gap between those seeking guidance and those providing it.

Finally, technology is playing an important role in the preservation of ancient Indian spiritual practices. Through digital archives, it is now possible to view Indian spiritual texts and recordings that date back hundreds of years. This not only helps preserve the ancient Indian traditions, but also enables modern Indians to gain insight into the past, allowing them to connect more deeply to their spiritual roots.

Technology has become an essential tool for modern Indian spiritualists, allowing them to access a deeper level of understanding and engage with religious ceremonies without having to travel. It has also made it easier to connect with teachers and spiritual guides, and to access ancient teachings, reminders, and texts. Technology may have its critics, but it has also helped ignite a new era of spiritual awakening in India, one that is bolstered by an unprecedented level of access to religious knowledge and information.

ᐅᐅᐅ

"India has a way of mesmerizing you, captivating you, and fascinating you. There's a magic to India that's hard to explain." - Anthony Bourdain

SIX

THE IMPACT OF WESTERNIZATION ON INDIAN SPIRITUALITY

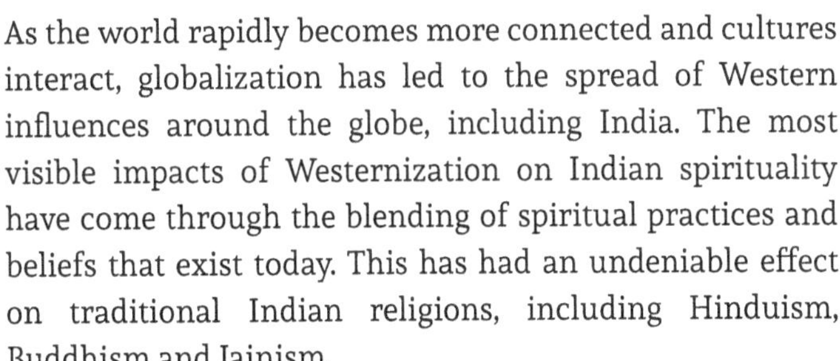

As the world rapidly becomes more connected and cultures interact, globalization has led to the spread of Western influences around the globe, including India. The most visible impacts of Westernization on Indian spirituality have come through the blending of spiritual practices and beliefs that exist today. This has had an undeniable effect on traditional Indian religions, including Hinduism, Buddhism and Jainism.

To begin with, in terms of traditional beliefs, the concept of God in India is highly abstract and spiritual. Meanwhile, the Abrahamic traditions of the Western world bring in an anthropomorphic depiction of God, which may be influencing a greater acceptance of this concept among traditionally religious people in India. Further, the emphasis on morality and certain religious rules present in the Western teachings can be witnessed in the jaded Indian faith, thereby touching the living religion that Hindus, Buddhists and Jains hold close to their hearts.

Moreover, the Western preoccupation with materialism has lessened the Indian focus on the inner self and its spiritual development. An increasing number of modern followers of Indian religions seek fulfillment through material accomplishments, comparing themselves with their more scientifically advanced counterparts. This is to the detriment of ancient spiritual practices that dwell on the exploration of the inner realm and the freeing of the soul from the confines of earthly attachments. Additionally, the search for material has led to the destruction of primitive forests, negating the land that is typical to the religious worship of Hinduism, Buddhism, and Jainism, as many places of worship no longer exist in their natural forms.

It can be disputed that the impact of Westernization on Indian spirituality has been more negative than positive. The weakening of traditional faiths and the emergence of materialism has led to the di- secularization of many temples, as well as the adoption of new-age practices that have no essential roots in Indian spirituality. This has caused discontent among many religious people, as more authentic rituals and meditations seem to be disappearing at an alarming rate.

The effect of Westernization on Indian spirituality is quite evident. The gradual merging of spiritual beliefs has weakened traditional faiths while creating an environment dominated by materialistic values. This has caused the destruction of sacred land and the diminishing presence of authentic spiritual practices. Therefore, it is important to recognize the essence of ancient Indian spirituality and make conscious efforts to keep these timeless practices alive.

ᤐᤐᤐ

"India is a land of ancient civilization and culture, where tradition and modernity coexist in perfect harmony." - Dalai Lama

SEVEN

The Role of Women in Modern Indian Spirituality

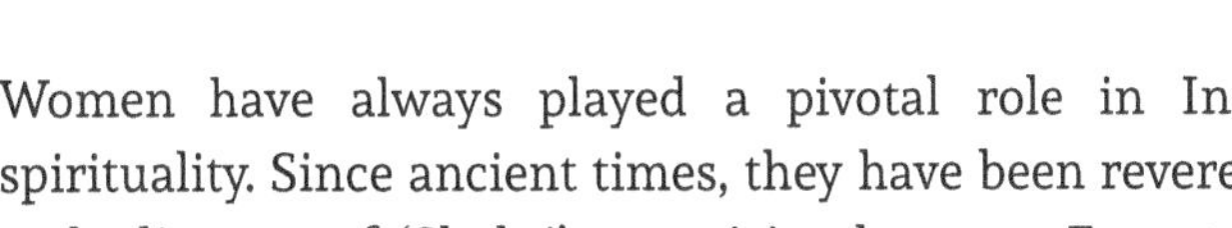

Women have always played a pivotal role in Indian spirituality. Since ancient times, they have been revered as embodiments of 'Shakti', or spiritual power. Even today, women form a major part of the religious landscape of 4 India, participating and leading spiritual movements that are transforming the nation.

One of the most encouraging developments in modern India is the emergence of female spiritual leaders, who are redefining spiritual practice and exploring new paths of spiritual empowerment. Among these women is Sadhvi Bhagawati Saraswati, who has become a powerful voice for social and spiritual change in India. Bhagawati is a Hindu nun and the founder of the Mata Amritanandamayi Math, a spiritual organization devoted to service, spiritual rejuvenation, and education. Bhagawati is an outspoken advocate for women and their spiritual potential, and has inspired other women to take up spiritual leadership roles in their communities.

Women are also forming communities to share their spiritual knowledge. Women's spiritual groups are popping up across the country, providing spaces for women to come together and discuss their spiritual journeys. These groups also provide mentorships and workshops to help new spiritual seekers find their footing, and they offer support and resources to help women become wiser and more empowered.

The world of modern Indian spirituality is also being shaped by female-centric technology. Online platforms such as „HolyGram and „RaagHive are connecting spiritual practitioners with online communities and resources, helping them to explore the spiritual realm and expand their horizons. These digital platforms are allowing women to share their spiritual experiences and knowledge in an open and accessible environment, thereby creating a spiritual landscape that is truly shaped by and for women.

Women have become an intrinsic part of modern Indian spirituality, and this trend is likely to continue. As more female spiritual leaders come to the fore and more women explore their spiritual potential, India will continue to evolve and develop a spiritually energizing and empowering environment for all.

ॐॐॐ

"India is the meeting place of the religions and among these Hinduism alone is by itself a vast and complex thing, not so much a religion as a great diversified and yet subtly unified mass of spiritual thought, realization and aspiration."
- Sri Aurobindo

EIGHT

THE INTERSECTION OF SCIENCE AND INDIAN SPIRITUALITY

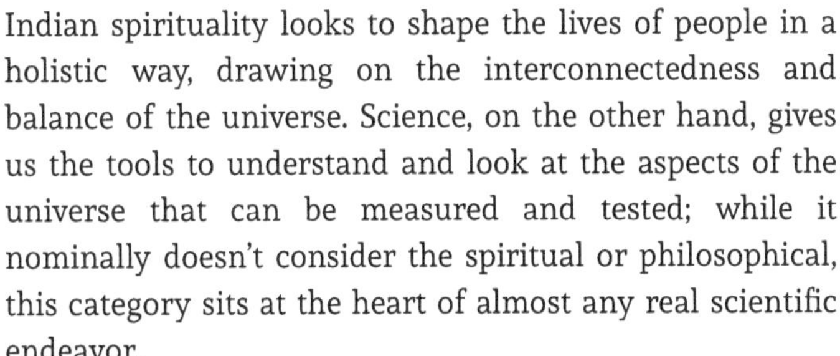

Indian spirituality looks to shape the lives of people in a holistic way, drawing on the interconnectedness and balance of the universe. Science, on the other hand, gives us the tools to understand and look at the aspects of the universe that can be measured and tested; while it nominally doesn't consider the spiritual or philosophical, this category sits at the heart of almost any real scientific endeavor.

At the point at which spirituality and science meet is perhaps the utmost area of potential understanding and exploration. While spirituality is best thought of as focusing more on a humbler, intuitive understanding of the universe and of ourselves and others, science tells us more about the workings of the universe on a deeper, more scientific level. Studying the intersection between science and spirituality could open up whole new understandings of being and matters seeking a more profound and deeper understanding.

The Indian spiritual tradition has long held a fascination for scientists and philosophers across the ages, from ancient Greece to the present day. Perhaps even more so in the present, many intellectuals have looked at the different paths of spirituality and science, viewing both in a holistic perspective that is uncoupled from the other. This is the essential element of understanding the validity and importance of both concepts, allowing the individual to step back and look at the bigger picture.

In Indian spirituality, there is no single answer to any given problem or situation, but rather a range of methodologies that one might use to try to come to understanding. These paths of understanding are often based on the most isometric spiritual understanding of the individual and the universe, which ties into a science that focuses more on experimentation and empirical study than the more abstract pathways of spirituality. Both concepts are highly influential, and the intersection of these two distinct fields is of great importance to understanding the complexity of the world around us.

It cannot be said that Indian spirituality should be judged solely by its scientific merits, nor should science be completely abstracted from its philosophical implications. Indian spirituality has been historically vibrant, and its closely related sciences still affect the lives of people from all walks of life. If a person is looking for a deeper, more meaningful understanding of their place in the universe, then looking at the intersection between science and Indian spirituality certainly offers a valuable path forward. Looking at both in their totality can provide a more comprehensive perspective on the world around us, allowing us the opportunity to make more informed decisions in the present and future.

ϸϸϸ

"In India, I found a race of mortals living upon the Earth, but not adhering to it." - Ralph Waldo Emerson

NINE

THE EVOLUTION OF HINDUISM IN THE 21ST CENTURY

Hinduism has been the major religion of the people of Indian subcontinent from time immemorial. Through the centuries, Hinduism has evolved in many ways, especially in the 21st century. Despite various challenges, Hindus have miraculously managed to adjust and incorporate changes in their ancient traditions.

In the 21st century, Hinduism has been evolving in terms of belief, practice and outlook. Most importantly, it underwent drastic changes particularly in the fields of science, technology, education and industrialization. As a result, many persons belonging to Hindu faith have become more scientific in their outlook and worldly in their perspective. They have started embracing agnostic and atheistic values which have made them open to discussing various points of view. This modern view of religion has been embraced by Vishwa-Hindu Parishad, one of the most influential Hindu organizations in India. This organization has promoted a culture of tolerance, equal-opportunity and development.

Furthermore, it has also tried to bridge the gap between traditional and modern values by insisting that modern educational opportunities and technological advancements should be available to all Hindus irrespective of their caste, gender and socio-economic status. This has made Hindus to aspire for higher economic, social and political goals.

Additionally, many temples and Hindu gatherings have also embraced modern technologies like internet and social media. This helps them to make their sacred rituals and preachings easily accessible to more people, which in turn strengthens the popularity of the religion. This has made a huge impact in helping people from far and remote places to be a part of the Hindu culture.

The 21st century has therefore been the era for rapid adoption worldwide for digital technologies and the internet. Hindus too have been quick in exploiting the potential of this digital transformation and have used it for spreading the bonds of their faith to wider circles of people. With its ever-evolving form and thought, Hinduism is on the path of becoming a global religion.

ᕤᕤᕤ

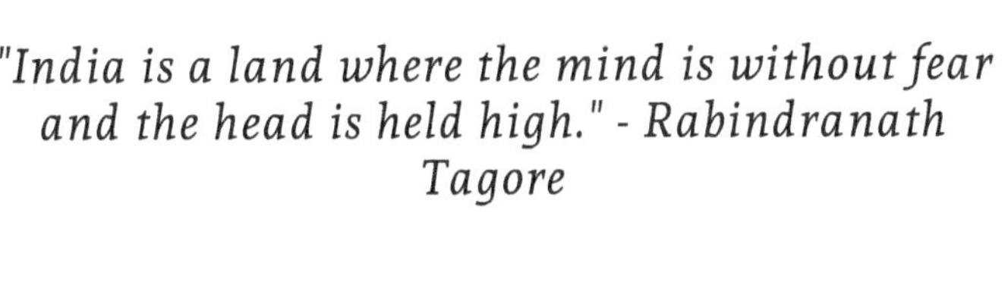
"India is a land where the mind is without fear
and the head is held high." - Rabindranath
Tagore

TEN

THE IMPACT OF CLIMATE CHANGE ON INDIAN SPIRITUALITY AND RELIGION

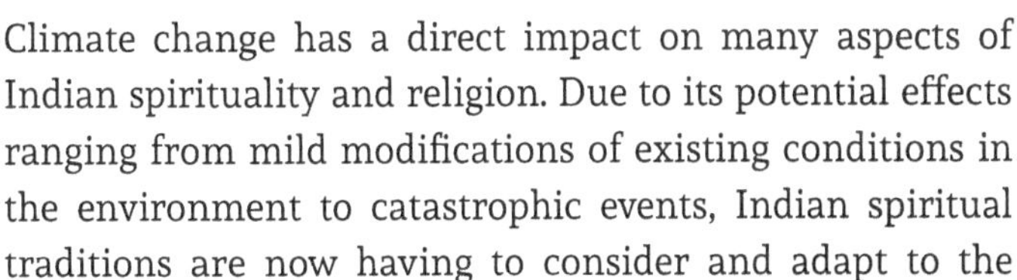

Climate change has a direct impact on many aspects of Indian spirituality and religion. Due to its potential effects ranging from mild modifications of existing conditions in the environment to catastrophic events, Indian spiritual traditions are now having to consider and adapt to the effects of climate change.

Religious and spiritual traditions such as Hinduism and Buddhism have long been linked to the worship of nature. The ancient Hindu epics, the Ramayana and the Mahabharata, laud the beauty and power of nature as exemplified by the Gods and Goddesses, who in turn are connected to various elements of the natural environment like clouds, rivers and trees. Hence, climate change and its effects can have a profound impact on the religious and spiritual practices of Hindus, particularly when it comes to their relationship with nature.

Heat waves, floods and droughts due to rising global temperatures have induced the displacement of millions of people in the Indian plains and the coastal areas. This displacement of peoples and resources can have an impact on the traditional pilgrimage routes, spiritual sites, and festivals that are vital to the expression of religious beliefs in India.

The rising sea levels and global temperatures have become a major environmental issue, as they can have a direct impact on Hindu spiritual practices. For example, some Hindu rituals, including vrata and devotional festivals, are traditionally performed near the coast, while such rituals may be rendered impossible if the sea levels continue to rise.

Additionally, deforestation has caused a massive decline in biodiversity, which in turn has led to a decrease in the variety of flora and fauna associated with Hinduism and its rituals. This has reduced the numbers of various species of birds, insects and animals, as well as plants, used for religious offerings and ceremonies.

The disruption and destruction of the natural environment by climate change has had a noticeable effect on Indian spirituality and its practices. This includes the decrease in the number of pilgrimages and festivals, changes in the traditional routes, and the harvesting of natural resources for rituals. Climate change has thus caused a shift in the spiritual experiences of many Hindu believers and practitioners. Despite this, due to the deep roots and resilience of Hinduism, these changes in nature have not caused an essential transformation of the faith. Rather, Hindus have adapted to the changing environmental conditions and have even incorporated climate change into their spiritual practices.

Climate change has had a significant impact on Hindu spirituality and religious traditions in India. Rising global temperatures, floods, droughts and deforestation have all played a role in changing the spiritual experiences of Hindus and their relationship to nature. However, these changes have not caused a fundamental shift in the faith of Hindus, as they have simply adapted and incorporated these changes into their spiritual practices.

ᐅᐅᐅ

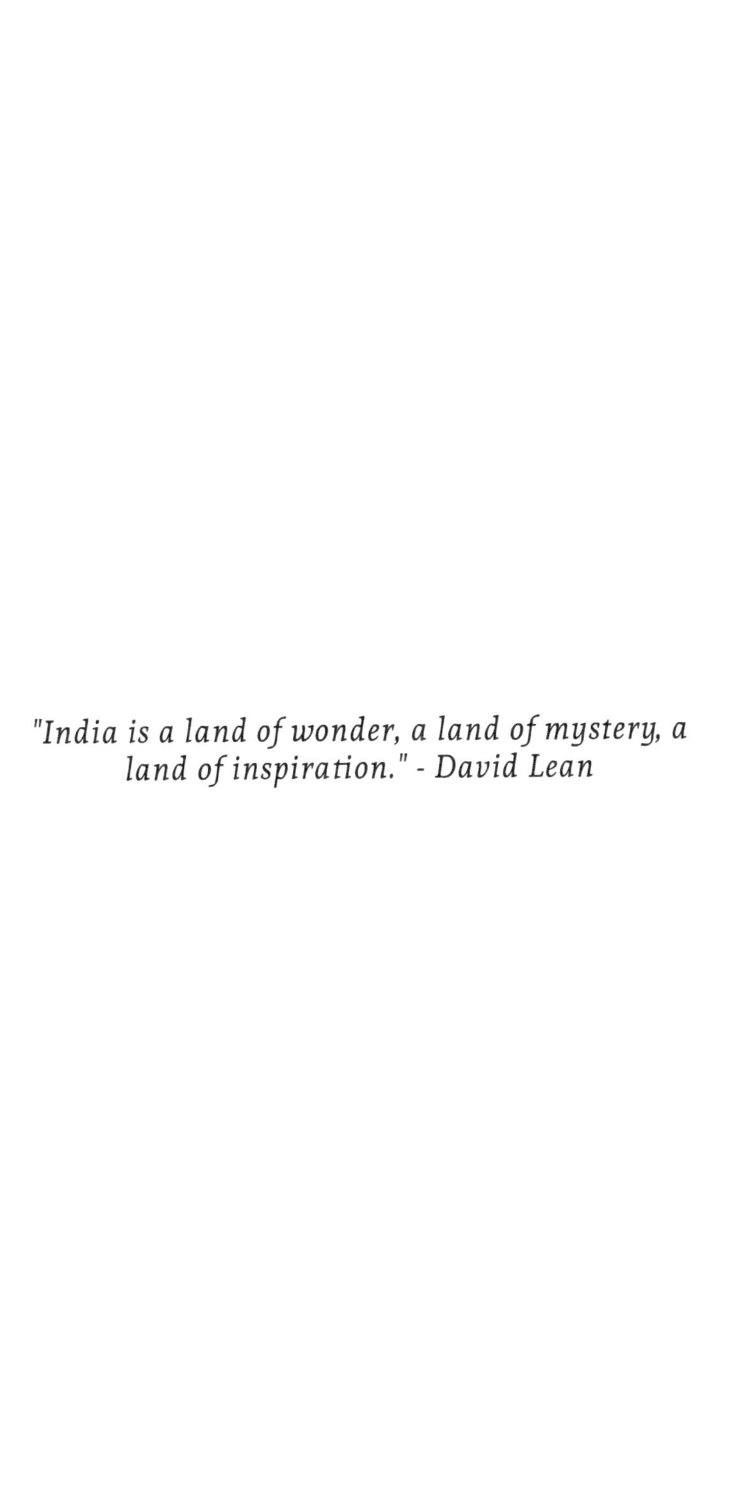

"India is a land of wonder, a land of mystery, a land of inspiration." - David Lean

ELEVEN

THE ROLE OF INDIAN SPIRITUALITY IN SOCIAL AND POLITICAL MOVEMENTS

India has a rich spiritual heritage that has shaped the nation's culture and ideology for centuries. As a result, spirituality has been a major factor in social and political movements throughout Indian history. From inspiring resistance against colonial occupation to adding a moral and ethical dimension to civil rights politics, Indian spirituality has shaped various social and political movements in the country.

Indian spirituality does not always advocate for or against specific political movements, but rather it serves as a framework for analyzing social issues and engaging in justice-based action. Many spiritual traditions such as Hinduism and Buddhism emphasize the importance of karma, or cause and effect, as a guide for social action. This spiritual view of the world encourages individuals to act in ways that result in positive change. As a result, Indian spirituality can serve as a powerful force for social change and help individuals bring about meaningful transformation in their communities.

Indian spirituality has been an important inspiration for many of the country's social and political movements throughout its history. The Bhakti movement of the 15th and 16th centuries, for example, was a major spiritual renewal movement in India that promoted an egalitarian religious system and fought against the oppressive structure of Hindu orthodoxy. Similarly, the Indian independence movement was also inspired by principles of Indian spirituality. Satyagraha, a nonviolent form of civil disobedience, was popularized by Mahatma Gandhi to promote independence from British rule. In this way, Indian spiritual traditions provided a moral and ethical framework for Indian people to oppose colonialism and fight for freedom.

Beyond inspiring direct political action, Indian spirituality has also helped create social conditions that are more conducive to justice-based movements. Hindu philosophical systems such as Advaita Vedanta emphasize the unity and inter-connectedness of all living beings and it is this understanding of an interconnected world that encourages people to work together to bring about positive change. Similarly, teachings of non-violence, compassion and selflessness in Indian spiritual traditions inspire individuals to act with a sense of responsibility towards the collective.

Indian spirituality has played an influential role in shaping social and political movements in the country. By providing a spiritual framework for understanding oppression and inequity, Indian spirituality has been both an important source of inspiration for justice-based initiatives and a powerful tool for transforming social conditions. As such, Indian spirituality continues to be an integral part of India's social and political life.

᭞᭞᭞

"India is the cradle of the human race, the birthplace of human speech, the mother of history, the grandmother of legend, and the great grandmother of tradition." - Mark Twain

Reference

|| Internet and various other books and scriptures from the Library Collectons ||

Other Books Of The Author

1. The Moments When I Met God
2. Kashiyile Theertha Pathangal
3. GURU GYAN VANI
4. Abhiprerak Gita
5. ASSI SE JAIN GHAT TAK
6. Hopelessness of Arjuna
7. The Soul and It's True Nature
8. Sense of Action (Karma)
9. Action through Wisdom
10. Action through Wisdom
11. THEORY AND PRACTICAL OF EVERY ACTION
12. LOGICAL UNDERSTANDING OF THE SUPREME
13. THE IMPERISHABLE SUPREME
14. Yatra Nishadraj se Hanuman Ghat Tak
15. Yatra Karnatak Ghat se Raja Ghat Tak
16. Yatra Pandey Ghat se Prayagraj Ghat Tak
17. Yatra Ranjendra Prasad Ghat se Dattatreya Ghat Tak
18. YaatraSindhiya Ghat se Gwaliar Ghat Tak
19. Yatra Mangala Gauri Ghat se Hanuman Gadhi Ghat Tak
20. Yatra Gaay Ghat Se Nishad Ghat Tak
21. MAA GANGA, GHATEN EVM UTSAV
22. Ganga Arti Dev Deepavali evam Any Utsav
23. Potentials of Digitalized India
24. VEDIC CONSCIOUSNESS
25. A Brief Introduction to Vedic Science
26. Kashi ke Barah Jyotirling
27. IMPACT OF MOTIVATION
28. Let's have a Milky Way Journey
29. Color Therapy in a Nutshell

ᗼᗼᗼ

Contact

DR. JAGADEESH PILLAI

PhD in Vedic Science

Four Times Guinness World Record Holder

Winner of Mahatma Gandhi Vishwa Shanti Puraskar and Global Peace Ambassador

Gemology, Astro & Vastu Consultant - Spiritual Counselor

Consultant for designing World Record Ideas

Efficient Tarot Card Reader

9839093003

myrichindia@gmail.com

drjagadeeshpillai@facebook

drjagadeeshpillai@instagram

jagadeeshpillai@youtube

www. JAGADEESHPILLAI.com

❧❧❧

|| LOKAHA SAMASTHAHA SUKHINO BHAVANTU ||

• 71 •